Budc

A Practical Guide to Integrating and Practicing Buddhism in Everyday Life

ISBN-10: 1523876824
ISBN-13: 978-1523876822

DEDICATION

For my brother, mom, and dad. Thanks for always
believing and supporting me along the way.

CONTENTS

1 INTRODUCTION

I want to thank you and congratulate you for purchasing the book, *"Buddhism: A Practical Guide to Integrating and Practicing Buddhism in Everyday Life"*.

This book contains proven steps and strategies on how to practice and make Buddhism a part of your daily activities.

One of the most prevalent and largely praised philosophies today, Buddhism is followed by millions of people all over the world. There are many conceptions of this philosophy, but it cannot be argued that Buddhism – for those who take its teachings seriously – find peace, wisdom, and rightness in their pursuance of the lifestyle. In this book, you'll find out exactly what Buddhism is and how you can apply the teachings of Buddha in your day to day life.

Thanks again for purchasing this book, I hope you enjoy it!

2 WHAT IS BUDDHISM?

Buddhism is a philosophy.

Contrary to what most people think, it is not a religion but rather, a way of living your life. Hailing from the teachings of Gautama Buddha, it is a pathway towards self-discovery, which in the process allows you to discover and connect with your surroundings. Buddhism is composed of traditions, beliefs, and spiritual practices done by Buddha himself.

There are two accepted branches of Buddhism: *Theravada* and *Mahayana*. Schools on Buddhism often practice just one form of teaching and you will find that the difference is typically geographical in nature. For example, Theravada is mainly practiced in Sri Lanka while Mahayana is more popular in South East Asia. Either way, both practices have for their purpose the same teachings or philosophy.

Theravada

Literally translated to School of the Elder Monks, Theravada promotes the practice of vibhajjavada or the *teaching of analysis*. The doctrine encourages insight that comes from the personal experience of the practitioner, followed by the application of their knowledge and critical reasoning. Although this might seem like something everyone is already doing, Theravada takes it one step further by teaching you the path to truly discovering yourself.

The basic outline of Theravada refers to the Seven Stages of Purification. Before starting on this path, however, you will first have to go through Learning, Practice, and eventually, Nirvana. These are essentially the concepts you will have to understand before you can undertake the Seven Stages of Purification.

Learning under the Theravada

There are the 3 Marks of Existence: Defilement, Ignorance, and Cause and Effect. These are essentially the different truths or concepts you will have to fully understand and accept before pursuing Buddhism. Without accepting these concepts, it will be harder for you to continue on the path to enlightenment.

The Three Marks of Existence

1. Annica or Impermanence – simply put, all conditioned phenomena will change and that nothing is permanent.

2. Dukkha or Suffering – suffering is caused by craving because people crave things that are

transitory, perishable, and changing. Since everything is transitory and changing, then craving anything may cause suffering. A person has this habit of labeling anything good, bad, comfortable and uncomfortable - and this will cause suffering on the part of the person. One must free himself from the need to label things as "like" or "dislike" in order to attain ultimate freedom. It is the object of the practice of Buddhism to help practitioners realize that the problem, cause, solution, and even implementation all start and come from oneself.

3. Anatta or Not Self – last we've got anatta or Not Self which at first might seem contradictory to the original goal of Buddhism. You must understand however that everything is transitory – even you. Hence, there is no 'true self' as described by anatta but rather, there are just five aggregates which compose every individual. These five aggregates are physical forms, feelings or sensations, perception, mental formations, and consciousness. There is no core aggregate or element, which means that all five of these are crucial to the buildup of a person. More importantly – all of these aggregates are changing and the goal of the Buddhist is to have a clear view of the process of change.

By understanding these *Three Marks of Existence*, you will be given insight into the world for the purpose of giving an end to suffering and eventually, the pathway to freedom. Learning also includes the *Four Noble Truths* which can be related to the *Three Marks of Existence*. The *Four Noble Truths* express the basic course of the philosophy, which is freedom from suffering through a path of liberation.

The Four Noble Truths

1. *Dukkha or Suffering* – classified into three categories, there's (1) inherent suffering, (2) suffering due to change, and (3) suffering through unrealization of the aggregates. Inherent suffering refers to the suffering that becomes evident in one's worldly activities. These are the sufferings you experience on a day to day basis whether they're disease, aging, birth, sadness, fear, pain, and others. It is those that you feel when you hate or when you separate yourself from the things you love.

    The second category is suffering due to change which proposes that detachment from things you find good or comfortable thereby causes suffering. Suffering, therefore starts from attachment and when detachment occurs – as all things must because of the transitory nature of existence – then the suffering becomes evident.

    The third one is the hardest of all categories to grasp because it is very subtle. It is called *Sankhara Dukkha* wherein people suffer *because* they have no grasp of the ever-present change. In this category, people do not realize that they do not have a core self but rather, have five aggregates composing their person.

2. *Dukkha Samudaya or Cause of Suffering* – this categorizes the different causes of suffering which includes Kama Tanha, Bhava Tanha, and Vibhaba Tanha. In general, Dukkha Samudaya talks about craving and attachment – all of which leads to suffering. The first one, Kama Tanha is the most basic relating to a craving of any pleasurable sense, particularly the five senses and mental perceptive. In the most basic sense, this may

include the craving for good food or the craving for success or distinction. The second one is Bhava Tanha, which talks about attachment to ongoing processes. Last is Vibhava Tanha, a craving for detachment from a process.

3. *Dukka Nirodha or the Cessation of Suffering* – in the cessation of suffering, the goal is to stop the craving entirely – which means that you'll have to detach yourself from the objects of your craving. This doesn't mean you should stop enjoying life's little pleasures but rather, understand that these are not necessary for your life.

4. *Dukkha Nirodha Gamini Patipada* – last is the pathway to Freedom from Suffering. This is where the Noble Eightfold Pathway comes in which eventually leads to Nirvana. In English, this translates to the rightness of your: view, intention, speech, actions, livelihood, effort, mindfulness, and concentration. More on the Noble Eightfold Pathway will be discussed later.

Defilement, Ignorance, and the Cause and Effect

The Defilements are seen by practitioners of Theravada to be the source of all evil, of all inhumanities which essentially makes it something that must be dispensed with. It is said to be the cause of existence and suffering that makes it impossible for a person to concentrate. It's actually a fivefold set called the *Five Hindrances* which can be further explained later.

For Theravada practitioners, the Hindrances cannot be defeated instantly. In fact, they come and go and it is in the interest of Buddhism to deal with them each time. There are three stages of Defilements which includes: Anusaya or Latent Tendencies, which exists as mental continuums, dormant until they reach the stage of Pariyutthana.

At the second stage, they manifest themselves through thoughts, volitions, and emotions. Lastly, there's the Vitikkama or Transgression wherein the bad thoughts are translated into actions or words. It is believed that these *Defilements* are caused by the *Ignorance* of people regarding their true selves. The ignorance consists of the belief that your true Self can be attached to your body when in truth, it is a transient being just like any other.

Practice and Nirvana under Theravada

Once you understand the *Learning* stage of Theravada Buddhism, it is time to move onto *Practice* that will eventually lead to *Nirvana*. However, those two instances will be explained later in the book.

Mahayana

Another popular extant of Buddhism is Mahayana or "The Great Vehicle" which is popularly followed in Southeast Asia. Compared to Mahayana, Theravada is often seen as a practice of less prominence in Buddhism. This is because Theravada is mainly practiced by laymen while Mahayana practitioners often take it one step further. A clear distinction between the two is that while Theravada focuses on the internal rightness of the person, Mahayana encompasses not just the practitioner but also other sentient beings. Loosely said, it is following the path of enlightenment for the benefit of all.

The Issue of Rebirth

This is also another common concept in Buddhism that is not entirely understood by others. The conventional belief is that Buddhists believes in rebirth or reincarnation. It is actually far deeper than that.

The concept of the Five Aggregates has already been discussed in this chapter and the philosophy of Buddhists and rebirth stems from these aggregates. It is believed that the aggregates are part of an evolving consciousness. Upon death, these aggregates are 'dissolved' and they become part of a stream of aggregates which essentially results in the formation of another collection of the Five Aggregates. The new person is neither different nor identical to the old one and such rebirth depends on Karma.

3 THE HISTORY OF BUDDHISM

Buddhism has a long and very colorful history that traces back to India. The story goes as far back as the 6th century BC from the birth of Siddhartha Gautama in Nepal. He is referred to as the Buddha or the Enlightened One.

The word Buddhism itself comes from the root word "Budhi", which is loosely translated to "to wake up". This is why the Buddha is called "The Enlightened One" because he has 'woken up' through the Buddhism philosophy. Today, this way of life is followed by more than 300 million people all over the world.

It is estimated that Buddhism is already 2,500 years old.

Misconceptions about Buddhism

As you probably know by now, when people refer to the Buddha, they usually mean Siddhartha Gautama who achieved the Enlightened State at the age of 35 years old. The problem with most people, however, is that they *think* Buddhism is a religion that worships the Buddha in the same way that Catholics worship their God. However, this is not the case at all.

In Buddhism, practitioners simply show their great respect for the Buddha and his teachings. After all, he is the one who first started it all and therefore, it is his teachings that are being used by others to follow the same path. In Buddhism, the ultimate goal of every person is to be enlightened and to awaken in much the same way as Siddhartha Gautama. Hence, Buddhism is a philosophy that helps people be Buddha's in themselves and the worship is given as a show of respect. There are no prayers offered to the Buddha in the hope that Gautama will answer their prayers.

The Spread of Buddhism

The Buddha Gautama had followers during his days and it was those followers that eventually established roots in different locations in order to further the teachings of Buddha. Settling in different regions, it was somewhat inevitable that the principles of Buddhism expanded well beyond its origins. Today, Buddhism is no longer confined to India or Asia but also in Western countries. Of course, the teachings of the Buddha can be somewhat hard to reconcile with the modern lifestyle, but it can be done.

4 HOW CAN BUDDHISM BENEFIT MY LIFE?

Yes, Buddhism can definitely benefit your life, not just in a general sense but in practically everything you do. In the general, day-to-day sense, you'll find that the philosophies extolled by Buddhism can be highly useful in keeping you on the mindful and useful path. Prior to going to those, however, we'll first talk about the ultimate benefit of Buddhism: Nirvana.

Attainment and Nirvana

Once you have gone through *Practice*, you will be able to achieve *Nirvana*. Practice is said to lead to Mundane Wisdom which rises from the Three Marks of Existence. Surpassing this, you ascend to the level of Supramundane which transcends the world as you know it.

Now, there are four levels of attainment and upon reaching the fourth level, you finally enter the state of Nirvana.

1. Stream Enterers – those who managed to destroy the first three fetter which include: false view of self, doubt, and the clinging to rites and rituals.

2. Once Returners – those who managed to also destroy the fetter of lust and hatred.

3. Non Returners – those who managed to destroy sensual desire and ill will. Destruction of these fretters will free a person from those that bind him to a world of senses.

4. Arahants – the enlightened ones, the same ones who reach Nirvana. This carries with it the state of deathlessness. They are free from ignorance, craving, and attachments with no chance of a rebirth of these sources of suffering.

Removal of Pain and Suffering

The three poisons are greed, hatred, and delusion. You'll find that by living and following the concepts of Buddhism, you will be able to remove these poisons from your life which are pinpointed to be the causes of suffering. In effect, this gives you the chance to embrace life happily and full of contentment with the knowledge that the future does not hold terror for you.

Embracing the Change

As already mentioned, one of the core concepts of Buddhism is that there is no One Self because we are all made up of aggregates that are constantly changing. This is the concept a lot of people struggle with because change is not something cherished by most people. We cling to constancy and any change, whether in the physical, emotional, mental, or spiritual bring about pain and suffering. The path of Buddhism, therefore, teaches you to *detach* yourself from the desire of forming attachments but rather, accept the ongoing and never-ending changes in life. Since attachment is viewed as the source of suffering, Buddhism will teach you to nip suffering in the bud by learning to ignore the cause.

Healthier Lifestyle

One of the benefits of a Buddhist lifestyle is health. Meditation, in particular, has been known to help individuals maintain a better mind and body. In meditation, you'll be able to find peace and essentially get rid of restlessness and the many sources of stress. There are studies that show how meditation can help regulate blood pressure, making it perfect for those who suffer from hypertension.

Connecting With Others

Contrary to what a lot of people seem to think, Buddhism doesn't foster being alone. It relishes on the quiet and may extol on the virtue of silence – but it doesn't really push people into living the antisocial lifestyle. In fact, Buddhism will promote connection with other people in a deeper, more understand kind of way. You will find yourself connecting better and understanding more of the human condition which naturally gives rise to compassion. You'll find that many Buddhists talk about compassion and make strides to help others although those actions are rarely advertised.

Contentment

Buddhism extols on the virtue of simplicity and being content with what you have. It promotes balance and essentially gives you the chance to get rid of greed, envy, desire, and other unhealthy emotions that prevent you from being content with what you have.

All in all, following the path of Buddhism, doesn't have just a single isolated benefit. The philosophy is a way of life and thereby is something that will affect every aspect of your life for the better. The benefits mentioned above are just mere glimpses of what you will be able to receive if you successfully live the way of the Buddhist or apply its teachings to daily life.

5 HOW CAN I APPLY BUDDHISM TO EVERYDAY LIFE?

Understanding the philosophy and the core concepts of Buddhism is the first step towards *Practice* with the intent of eventually achieving Nirvana. In this Chapter, we'll talk about the different methods of *Practice* under the Theravada because it is the most exhaustive one available. The *Mahayana* system will also be discussed later but since it is a deeper teaching of Buddhism, it will not be discussed in detail.

Seven Stages of Purification

The Seven Stages of Purification is the core framework followed in Theravada, the stages eventually leading to the concepts discussed in Chapter One: The Three Marks of Existence. Through the Stages, you'll be able to fully understand that Marks, remove ignorance in your life, and become enlightened.

1. Purification of Conduct

2. Purification of Mind

3. Purification of View

4. Purification by Overcoming Doubt

5. Purification by Knowledge and Vision of What is Path and Not Path

6. Purification by Knowledge and Vision of the Course of the Practice

   - Knowledge of contemplation of rise and fall

   - Knowledge of contemplation of dissolution

   - Knowledge of appearance as terror

   - Knowledge of contemplation of danger

   - Knowledge of contemplation of dispassion

   - Knowledge of desire for deliverance

   - Knowledge of contemplation of reflection

   - Knowledge of equanimity about formations

   - Conformity knowledge

7. Purification by knowledge and vision

   - Change of lineage

- ◆ The first path and fruit

- ◆ The second path and fruit

- ◆ The third path and fruit

- ◆ The fourth path and fruit

How to Use the Seven Stages

The Seven Stages are essentially a guideline as to where you would start when following the Buddhist path. The first few stages are pretty self-explanatory and should help you with your initial path. As you delve deeper in Buddhism however, you're going to need more than just basic and knowledge and instead get one-on-one teaching. This is especially true during the 6th stage which comes with sub-stages that need an experienced and invested guide to help you.

The Eight Fold Path

The Eight Fold Path is another important concept of the Buddhism philosophy. It's actually encompassed in the fourth of the **Four Noble Truths.** It is depicted by an eight-spoke wheel which represents every path in the philosophy. As extensive as it is, we'll try to make the explanation of the Eight Fold Path as simple as possible:

1. Right View – this is defined as the right way of seeing things. The Right View leaves you detached when viewing life, essentially separating your insights from holding any attitude, right or wrong.

2. Right Intention – in the right intention, a practitioner is coaxed into following the correct

path. It is the intention to rid yourself of wrong and immoral thoughts or those that will lead or cause suffering.

3. Right Speech – pretty explanatory, this is the proper way to talk, devoid of any evil intentions or ideas.

4. Right Action – following the Right Speech, Right Action extols on the virtues of deliberate movement. It also prevents one from doing wrong, immoral, or evil things such as taking a life, stealing, and hitting someone.

5. Right Livelihood – this is where things get complicated. Right livelihood essentially means distancing yourself from instances, actions, and surroundings that are evil and immoral. In the simplest sense, it means engaging in a way of living that does not endanger other people, whether directly or indirectly.

6. Right Effort – this path puts a value on persistence and diligence. It is not enough that you have chosen to start following the Right Path, what is important is that you continue to do so and make every effort not to stray from the path you have chosen. It is submitted that you will fail or be diverted at some point, but this should not discourage you in the least.

7. Right Mindfulness – this is the second to the last stage and contemplates both the present and the future. In this path, the practitioner is kept mindful and alert about the different external phenomena that could affect the body. Remember that Buddhist put much value in being stable so any external stimuli that could affect that stability must be considered and adjusted to. This is where

mindfulness comes in as you maintain readiness for any changes and accept them as they come.

8. Right of Concentration – finally, we come to the last stage. The Right of Concentration extols on the virtue of concentration. More specifically, it talks about the right way to meditate. Buddhist monks may spend hours meditating because this offers them a kind of insight unlike anything else. In a state of concentration or meditation, a monk is said to be aloof from all desires and unwholesome thoughts and accompanied by sustained thought, joy, and bliss.

Meditation and How to Practice It

Buddhists often dedicate a chunk of their lives following the teachings of Buddha. Even if you don't actually go the whole nine yards, however, you'll find that everyday use and application of the teachings of Buddha will help you towards the path of enlightenment.

Meditation is by far the easiest practice you can do that is promoted in Buddhism. That is not to say that meditation itself is easy – it's not. However, meditation is the one thing you can do immediately and practice on a daily basis until you get it right.

Now, the Buddha taught different kinds and techniques for meditation, but this book will focus on the two most common methods: the Mindfulness of Breathing and Loving Kindness Meditation.

Mindfulness of Breathing

Meditation, for the most part, follows the 4P rule which stands for place, posture, practice, and problems.

Place

Place refers to the location of your meditation. It doesn't have to be anywhere fancy or close to nature. Sometimes, it can be inside your room or your office. The point is that it should be somewhere where you feel completely relaxed and won't be disturbed for the next 10 minutes or so, depending on how long your meditation usually lasts.

Posture

You often see people meditating with their legs tucked together in a 'lotus' position. Now, the lotus position is actually hard to pull off, especially for a complete beginner. You may try the 'semi lotus' position or just bend your knees backward and keep your feet tucked under your bottom. The back should be kept straight – this will ensure that you maintain proper posture and that you won't get too tired or fall asleep in the middle of meditation.

Practice

Practice is when the meditation starts and in words, the practice seems easy enough. You will have to settle in your position, close your eyes, and focus on making slow, consistent, and even breaths. If you are having a hard time, try using these techniques:

- Inhale and exhale, then count one. Inhale and exhale then count two and so on until you get to ten. When you reach ten, start from the beginning.

- Count one for an inhale and two for an exhale. Repeat

- Focus on the movement of your abdomen as it rises and falls with each breath

- Visualize a ball in front of you that rises each time you breathe in and falls each time you breathe out

Problems

Ideally, you will practice meditation for a minimum of 7 minutes as a rank beginner. As you improve, however, you'll find yourself meditating at least 45 minutes each day. When starting, you'll find yourself tackling some problems in the middle of meditation. Common issues include discomfort in your position, itching, sudden thoughts entering your head, and various other issues. To solve this problem, you have to switch back your attention to your breath every time an issue arises. Now, this will happen several times for each session but you'll find that with patience and persistence, the problems will start to weaken, allowing you to practice meditation at a longer and more comfortable pace.

Loving Kindness Meditation

Loving Kindness Meditation should only be attempted only after you've mastered the Mindfulness of Breathing meditation. As the name suggests, it is the kind of meditation you go through when you want to promote or cultivate the virtues of love and kindness in your person. It is a kind of meditation that extends not just to your inner self but to everyone as well.

Now, meditation is by far the best way to get started when it comes to Buddhism. In some instances, there are those who practice meditation only without connecting it to the philosophy of Buddhism. You'll find that although it is possible, Meditation is best sought out in line with the virtues and teachings of the philosophy. This way, your meditations would be that much deeper, meaningful and deliberate.

Decluttering of Your Life

Here's something you should know about Gautama – he was born a prince or a member of royalty. This means that he could have lived in splendor and yet he restrained himself to only the most basic needs of life.

This is one way to follow the teachings of Buddha – separating yourself from the inessentials and focusing on what matters. You de-clutter yourself and essentially pursue a minimalist lifestyle. Now, this doesn't mean that you'll have to get rid of everything you own – just those that are redundant and unnecessary in your life.

How do you know if something is unnecessary or redundant? Try not using something for a whole week. Were you able to do it? Do you think you can do it for the next months or even year? If so, then perhaps you're better off without these things.

Decluttering your life means that you can stop worrying about them and their maintenance. With no car to speak of, you don't have to worry about renewing the registration, traffic, or the insurance for the vehicle. This frees up your mind from attachment and helps cut back on the source of suffering.

Now, there's actually a concept today that is in line with de-cluttering. It's called Minimalism and a lot of people are doing and using it today to make their lives simpler. Combined with the philosophies of Buddhism, you'll find that this way of life gives you a different kind of freedom.

Understand that All Shall Pass

In learning, it has been repeatedly said that everything is transitory and that change is inevitable. Now, this is a philosophy that you'll have to fully accept if you want to apply Buddhism in your daily life. Are you angry? Tired? Sad? Frustrated? Understand that these shall all pass at the right time. Although you might not be able to instantly remove suffering from your life, you are in the position to accept that they are there and those too, shall pass.

Be Deliberate on Tasks

Practically everything is a form of meditation if you do it properly, which is why even when performing tasks, you should be mindful of the actions you're taking. Do NOT multitask. Instead, devote all your attention towards the particular action you're doing. If you're washing dishes, wash dishes deliberately. Feel the movement of the sponge as you wipe it against the dishes, lather the soap, and be mindful of the water as it removes the soap suds off dishware. This might sound weird, but Buddhism puts a strong emphasis on being dedicated on what you are doing – no matter the time or place. Remember: if you cannot focus completely on a task, then how can you properly meditate?

Make Time and Remain Patient

Develop rituals and make time for certain things – such as meditation. It should be part of your goal to create consistent timelines or moments for doing certain things. This works much like an extension of meditation wherein you deliberately make time and deliberately perform tasks with the knowledge that you are meant to do these particular things at this particular time.

Failure is Acceptable

No one who has decided to follow the teachings of Buddhism managed to perfect it on the first try. Understand that failure is an acceptable path of life – not just in your practice of meditations but in every other aspect. Furthermore, failure is fleeting and such as with the concept of non-permanence, failure may be CHANGED. In fact, failure is equivalent to growth.

Be Present

This is a term loosely bandied about every time – but what exactly does it mean? Being present means paying close attention to what is happening around you. When you are with friends - then listen to what they have to say. When you are reading a book – then make sure that you are fully taking in the contents of the book. In modern times, this can be called 'not multitasking' but being present is actually deeper than that. It encompasses not just your 'presence' when with other people, but also 'presence' when you're alone.

Fear and Happiness Comes from Within

A valuable lesson taught by Buddhism is that everything comes from and in you. Fear and happiness are simply reactions to external elements and these reactions come from inside you. Hence, you have it within your power to control these reactions. If happiness and fear come from inside you, then you have the capacity to stop the fear and generate happiness without relying on books, movies, food and whatever it is that you used to rely on.

Forget What Other People Think

The problem with the modern lifestyle is that people are too invested in what other people are thinking. Upon learning Buddhism, this should not be the case. Detach your ego and stop thinking about what other people might be saying about you. Instead, focus on what you believe is important. Remember that every move, decision, and word you utter should be deliberate or with purpose, and that purpose should be aligned with the Rightness of the teachings of Buddhism. If you find that what you are doing is contrary to the teachings or something purely done for the benefit of what others think about you, then it's time to stop.

Of course, those are just a few of the things that you can do that reflect the Buddhist philosophies. Buddhism may be applied to everything in your life, so whenever you find yourself unsure about what to do next, just go back to the core concepts of Buddhism and follow the path laid down for you.

The only problem for modern followers of Buddhism philosophy is that they can be tough to incorporate into your day to day life. By this, we mean the modern lifestyle where everything seems to be fast and instant.

The good news is that there are people today who can help you with this path. Monks who are true to the way of Buddha are scattered all over the world, thereby giving you refuge should you want to truly understand his teachings and eventually reach Nirvana. You'll find that there are also papers and scriptures that further explain Buddhism. Remember, the philosophy was developed in a span of 2,500 years – you can't expect to learn everything about this way of life in just a short span of time.

Some of the best sources of additional Buddhism information can be found in the Pali Canon or the Tipitaka. If you can find an edition of this in English, it would be best to read it and fully immerse yourself into the way of the Buddhist.

6 CONCLUSION

Thank you again for downloading this book!

I hope this book was able to help you understand the philosophy of Buddhism.

The next step is to follow the instructions offered above and find the path toward Nirvana.

Finally, if you enjoyed this book, then I'd like to ask you for a favor, would you be kind enough to share this book with your friends and family? It'd be greatly appreciated!

Thank you and good luck!

ABOUT THE AUTHOR

Will Huynh is a life long learner. He is passionate about self-improvement and helping others. Currently, he works as a lead software engineer for a top tech company in the Silicon Valley. In his free time, he enjoys doing yoga, exercising, traveling, reading, and is currently learning Japanese for fun.

Printed in Great Britain
by Amazon